FOOTBALL EDITION

TIA ROGHAAR

For permission requests, contact:

Ryan Roghaar
info@r2mg.com
R2 Media Group Publications
Farmington, UT 84025

ISBN: 978-0-9824587-4-7
ITEM NUMBER: TMPB001-FOOTBALL
First Edition: 2025

All efforts have been made to ensure the accuracy of the information presented. Any opinions expressed are those of the author and do not necessarily reflect the views of the publisher.

Disclaimer
This publication is designed to provide general information and is not intended to serve as legal, financial, medical, or professional advice. The author and publisher disclaim any liability arising directly or indirectly from the use or application of this material. Readers should consult the appropriate professionals regarding their specific situations.

Printed in the United States of America.

Also available in the Team Mom Playbook series:

Team Mom Playbook: Football *Team Mom Playbook: Hockey*

Team Mom Playbook: Baseball *Team Mom Playbook: Soccer*

Team Mom Playbook: Softball *Team Mom Playbook: Lacrosse*

Team Mom Playbook: Basketball

Produced with support from:

goliathsportsmarketing.com

r2mg.com

Welcome to the Club!

Before we dive in, let's talk about the secret sauce to making this season and every season unforgettable: **community**. This guide is packed with tips and tools, but the real magic happens when you connect with other Team Moms. Share ideas, ask questions, and make friends who get it. Join our online community—it's free, fun, and full of support.

Shoot me an email if the link doesn't work or if you get lost along the way: **tia@teammomplaybook.com**.

Or click here:
https://community.teammomplaybook.com

Oh and one more thing...

I know there are team dads, grandparents, and other rockstar caregivers stepping up to fill the Team Mom role. That's awesome! At the end of the day, we're all here for the same reason: to make sure our kids have a season they'll never forget. For simplicity, I'll use "Team Mom" throughout this guide, but whoever you are—**THANK YOU.** You're part of the team, and we're thrilled to have you here.

Team Mom
PLAYBOOK

Disclaimer

Some links in this guide, now or in the future, may be affiliate links, meaning we earn a small commission if you use them. But here's the deal: I only recommend products and services I've personally vetted and love. You won't pay extra—in fact, you might even snag a discount. That said, feel free to do your own research or skip the links altogether. No pressure, just options.

Affiliate links are marked with this symbol: "$"

Contents

Section VIII: What's Next (cont.)

Section IX: Ending on a High Note

Section X: Sample Documents

Download digital versions of these forms and more at: **teammomplaybook.com/premium-forms**

Team Mom
PLAYBOOK

An Introduction to Team-Momming

What is a Team Mom?

> Team Mom tēm • mäm
> **(noun)**
>
> The center of your football universe. The individual without whom nothing gets done, snacks don't get eaten, and parties don't get planned. All seeing, all knowing, and your number one fan.
>
> SEE ALSO: Indispensable, Integral, Dependable

Let's talk about the MVP of any football team: **the Team Mom.** (Yes, I said it. Cue the gasps.) But seriously, this role is everything. Without a rockstar Team Mom, the team can fall apart faster than a cheap lawn chair. You're the glue holding everything together—making sure everyone knows where to be, when to be there, and what to bring. (And let's be real, for some kids, the post-game snack is the only reason they show up 😂.)

From organizing team dinners to coordinating end-of-season banquets, the Team Mom's job is equal parts logistics and love. It's a big job, but don't worry—this playbook is here to help. Whether you're a seasoned pro or a first-timer, you've got this.

Sure, but Why Bother?

Let me start by saying I absolutely love being a boy mom (times two—ages 14 and 18). But more than that, I'm a "mom" to entire teams of kids. Over the past decade, I've watched players grow, celebrated their wins, and hugged them after tough losses. Some of those kiddos still run across the field after high school games for a big, sweaty, stinky hug—and honestly, nothing makes me happier.

My boys? They're "embarrassed" by their mom shouting from the stands. (Secretly, though, they're proud. They'd just never admit it.)

What This Playbook Offers

Think of this as your ultimate toolkit. Over the years, I've accumulated plenty of tips, strategies, and lessons (some learned the hard way) that I'll share with you here. While this guide may not have everything (there's always room to grow and learn), it's a solid starting point. And hey, if you've got a game-changing strategy, don't keep it to yourself—join our online community and share it with other Team Moms. Together, we're stronger!

The Keys to Team Mom Success

To thrive in this role, you'll need to embrace a few core qualities:

- **Organization:** Your superpower. From schedules to snack sign-ups, you're the master planner.

- **Communication:** Clear, concise, and consistent. You're the bridge between coaches, parents, and players.

- **Empathy:** You're the heart of the team, always ready to lend an ear or a hand.

- **Adaptability:** Because, let's face it, plans change—and you're ready to pivot.

- **Passion:** Your love for the game and the team is contagious.

A Final Note Before We Dive In

Team Momming isn't always easy, but it's incredibly rewarding. The bonds you build and the memories you create will last a lifetime. So, take a deep breath, get ready to tackle the season, and remember—you're not alone. We've got a whole community cheering for you. **Let's make this the best season yet!**

Team Organization

Get Busy, Get Organized!

From the moment you raise your hand to become Team Mom, you're officially part of a sacred sorority of super-parents. Your mission? To ensure the team runs like a well-oiled machine. It takes a lot of work, but lets dig into how to make it happen.

Communication is Key

Clear and consistent communication ensures that coaches can focus on coaching, players can focus on playing, and parents can focus on supporting the team. Here are your main tools:

- **Group Texts:** Easy to set up, but limited functionality. Great for smaller teams.

- **Group Emails:** Perfect for sharing attachments, but not ideal for ongoing updates.

- **Team Apps:** Apps like **TeamSnap**, **GroupMe**, and **Band** offer robust features tailored for team organization. Here's how they stack up:

  - **TeamSnap:** My personal favorite! With options for scheduling, sign-ups, and photo sharing, it's worth the $9.99/month investment. Its intuitive interface keeps everyone in sync.

  - **GroupMe:** A text-based app with added features like private messaging, polls, and calendar events. Great for mid-sized teams but slightly less feature-rich than TeamSnap.

  - **Band:** Ideal for larger groups, this app allows unlimited participants, live video feeds, and robust calendar management. Perfect for high school teams or leagues.

Pro Tip: Test these apps using their free trial or basic tier to find what suits your team best.

TIME OUT!!

These are a few of my favorite team communication tools. Do you have one you like?

The Pre-Season Playbook

Preparation starts long before the first whistle blows. Use this checklist to ensure a smooth kick-off:

- [ ] **Create a Master Calendar:** Plot every practice, game, and event on a massive whiteboard or digital calendar. Include uniform deadlines, fundraising events, and tentative dates for team dinners and activities.

  Example: Use Google Calendar or a physical planner to keep track of all important dates.

- [ ] **Establish Communication Channels:** Choose your primary communication method and set expectations with parents and coaches during your first meeting. Make sure everyone knows how to stay updated.

  Example: If using TeamSnap, create a tutorial or guide for parents to help them navigate the app.

- [ ] **Delegate Early:** Find a tech-savvy parent to manage app sign-ups or a super-organized volunteer to coordinate snacks. Delegating builds a sense of ownership among parents and lightens your load.

  Example: Assign roles like "Snack Coordinator," "Fundraising Lead," and "Team Photographer" to different parents.

- [ ] **Gear Management:** Keeping track of gear can be one of the trickiest parts of the season. A few tips:

  - **Label Everything:** From water bottles to practice cones, clear labeling prevents mix-ups.

  - **Uniform Distribution:** Set up a clear system for handing out and collecting uniforms. Consider assigning a volunteer to oversee this process.

  - **Create a Lost-and-Found Bin:** Encourage players to check it regularly to avoid last-minute panics.

- [ ] **Managing the Team Budget:** Transparency and planning are essential when dealing with finances. Here's how to handle it:

  - **Draft a Budget:** Share an itemized budget with parents early in the season. Include expenses like team dinners, end-of-season gifts, and app subscriptions.

- **Collect Payments:** Use tools like Venmo or PayPal for easy tracking. For cash or check payments, maintain a simple log for accountability.

  Pro Tip: Keep receipts organized in a dedicated binder or folder.

- [ ] **Emergency Preparedness:** Football seasons can be unpredictable, so it's crucial to plan for the unexpected:

  - **First-Aid Kit:** Stock it with essentials and ensure it's always on hand.

  - **Helmet/equipment repair kit:** Stock this with appropriate snaps, screws, tools, and miscellaneous other parts to put helmets and other gear back together again when face masks fall off or chin straps go flying.

    Pro Tip: Keep a handful of extra mouth guards on hand for when the guys, drop them, lose them, leave them, or chew them up. They don't need to be fancy; they just need to work. You can always easily find these at your local Dick's Sporting Goods — or whatever you've got — or online.

  - **Emergency Contacts:** Keep a list of player emergency contacts easily accessible.

  - **Weather Plans:** Have a backup plan for practice or games affected by weather changes.

- [ ] **Celebrate Small Wins:** Success isn't just about wins on the scoreboard. Celebrate milestones like a player's first touchdown or a successful fundraiser. Recognizing these moments builds morale and fosters a positive team culture.

Example Pre-Season Timeline

Here's a sample timeline to help you stay on track:

6-8 Weeks Before Season Starts:

- [ ] Meet with coaches to discuss goals and expectations.
- [ ] Create a master calendar with all key dates.
- [ ] Set up communication channels and delegate roles.

4-5 Weeks Before Season Starts:

- [ ] Send out a welcome email to parents with important information and deadlines.
- [ ] Organize a uniform fitting and distribution day.
- [ ] Start collecting player fees and donations.

2-3 Weeks Before Season Starts:

- [ ] Finalize the team roster and share it with parents.
- [ ] Plan and schedule team-building activities, like a family BBQ or meet-and-greet.
- [ ] Confirm all volunteer roles and responsibilities.

1 Week Before Season Starts:

- [ ] Host a pre-season meeting with parents and players to go over the schedule, expectations, and any last-minute details.
- [ ] Double-check all equipment and supplies.
- [ ] Send out a final reminder with all the information parents and players need for the first practice.

Why it Matters

By organizing effectively and fostering clear communication, you'll set the stage for a smooth, successful season. The pre-season playbook is your roadmap to ensuring everyone is on the same page and ready to hit the ground running.

Team Building

Teamwork Makes the Dream Work

A successful team isn't just a group of players—it's a family. When players feel connected like siblings, and coaches become trusted mentors, the magic happens. Building that sense of unity requires commitment and effort from everyone, but it's often the Team Mom who takes the lead in fostering these connections. Whether it's through shared meals, team activities, or heartfelt moments, creating a bond off the field strengthens the team on the field.

As part of the team budget I establish at the beginning of the season, I earmark some money to cover the costs of plastic utensils, paper plates, cups, napkins, etc. Then, throughout the season I keep a tote in my car with all that stuff inside. So any time we're dining together — from treats and parties to team dinners — I share the supplies with the M.O.C. (Mom in Charge) of the meal and one more things is handled quickly and efficiently.

Half-Time and Post-Game Treats

Organizing snacks may seem like a small task, but it's one of the easiest ways to bring parents into the fold while ensuring players stay energized. Here's how to manage it effectively:

- **Use a Sign-Up Tool:** Platforms like **SignUp Genius** simplify snack scheduling. Parents can choose dates that work for them, and automatic reminders reduce no-shows.

  Don't want a tech solution? A simple PDF can work just fine, <insert PDF>.

- **Assign Roles in TeamSnap:** Sync the snack schedule with TeamSnap or your chosen app to keep everything centralized. Parents will appreciate having all information in one place.

SignUp Genius is a powerful tool for collaborating on meals and other activities.

- **Prioritize Healthy Options:** Encourage parents to provide healthy snacks for half-time, like fresh fruit or granola bars. Save the sugary treats for post-game celebrations.

- **Streamline Distribution:** Pre-pack individual servings in sandwich bags to make it easy for players to grab and go.

Not everyone does a half-time treat, but if you do, I encourage parents to provide a healthy mid-game snack — especially for the little ones. Post-game, the kids can go "hog wild" eating whatever they like, but at half-time it is really important that kiddos get a healthy boost.

I have found fresh fruit to be among the favorites. I will often wash and cut the fruit the night before, or morning of. I then put servings into individual sandwich bags. This allows players to grab what they want while coaches are talking. Kiddos can also put their garbage back in the sandwich bags, which makes clean-up a breeze.

Pro Tip: Be sure to pack a garbage bag with you so that the kiddos can easily pick-up after themselves — or more likely, you after them. :)

Team Dinners

Some of my fondest memories from my son's peewee football years came during team dinners. Typically, we'd host a team meal once a week, the Monday after the previous Saturday's game day. The purpose is to build camaraderie between the kids, their coaching staff, and their extended football family,

13

and for time infinitum sharing meals is one way people have done that.

- **Plan Ahead:** Use SignUp Genius or a simple PDF to organize the dinner schedule. Assign roles like main dish, side dish, drinks, and dessert to different families.

- **Keep It Simple:** Team dinners don't have to be fancy. Taco bars, spaghetti, baked potatoes, or even pizza nights work perfectly.

- **Set Up a Supply Tote:** Keep utensils, paper plates, napkins, and cups in a designated tote for easy access on dinner nights. It's a small detail that makes a big difference.

- **Involve the Coaches:** Inviting coaches to team dinners builds trust and helps players see them as approachable role models. They can also capitalize on this "quiet time" with the team to talk strategy or even review film. I joke though, team dinners are rarely "quiet time."

Team dinners don't have to be fancy. Players are often so ravenous after practice that they would literally eat anything. **The key here is to ask for help! The same people should not be feeding the kiddos and coaches every week.** I normally have one family provide drinks, another a side dish, another a simple desert, and perhaps one or multiple families supply the main dish. You may have to vary your count based on team size and economic factors, but the goal is to make team dinner a great experience for everyone, not a financial burden to any one family.

A consideration: It's sad to think about, but depending on the economic makeup of your team, it's possible that for some kids on your team this meal might be the only one they can count on. So, when the opportunity presents itself, any leftovers that haven't been fingered to death by everyone can be sent home with players or families who might want to, or need to, take them home.

Other Team-Building Activities

Team dinners and snacks are just the beginning. Here are some additional activities to foster unity and create lasting memories:

- **Family BBQs:** Kick off the season with a family barbecue. It's a great way for players and parents to mingle before the

Team dinners are great before game day. **Pool parties are not.**

Our only loss one year came after a celebratory pool party that left the kids flat and tired the following morning. It was a great night, but a hard loss. **Think ahead when planning activites before game day!**

schedule gets hectic. Add a fun element like water balloons or yard games to break the ice.

- **Dinner and Cornhole:** Host a casual evening at a local park with grills for burgers and hot dogs. Bring along a few cornhole sets and organize a mini-tournament. It's simple, affordable, and always a hit.

- **Bowling Nights:** Reserve a few lanes at a local bowling alley and let the team unwind. Mid-week or pre-season dates work best to avoid crowds. Pair it with pizza for an easy, crowd-pleasing activity.

- **Swimming Parties:** If you're lucky enough to have access to a pool, this can be a fun team-building option.

Encouraging Unity

Team building is about more than just activities—it's about creating a culture. Here are a few extra ways to nurture connection:

- **Create a Team Slogan or Mascot:** Rally the team around a shared identity. Host a contest to come up with a slogan or design, and use it on banners, shirts, or signs.

- **Celebrate Achievements:** Acknowledge both big and small victories. Did a player make their first tackle? Score their first touchdown? Celebrate it!

- **Involve Siblings and Parents:** Siblings and parents are part of the team too. Plan events that include the whole family to strengthen connections.

- **Volunteer Together:** Organize a community service day. Working together off the field is a powerful way to build camaraderie and give back.

Why It Matters

Unity transforms a team from a group of individuals into a cohesive force. It's what turns games into unforgettable experiences and creates lifelong memories for players and families alike. By prioritizing connection and camaraderie, you'll ensure the season is not only successful but meaningful for everyone involved.

Team Mom
PLAYBOOK

Who's Buying?

Let's Talk Money

Managing team finances can feel daunting, but it doesn't have to be. Transparency is your best friend, and a little organization goes a long way. Treat all team funds as if you're running a small business—keep them separate from your personal money, save every receipt, and always communicate clearly with parents. Remember, we're all in this for the same reason: to give our kids a great experience.

Budgeting Basics

I always start the season by coordinating with the coaches to hold a team meeting where I can share the detailed budget with parents. This meeting is an opportunity to clearly show how their money will be spent and to address any questions upfront, avoiding misunderstandings later. The budget (see attached sample) serves as a roadmap for covering all season costs, ensuring everyone understands where their contributions are going.

During the meeting, I outline the payment options available to parents, including cash, checks, or digital payments like Venmo. Personally, I prefer Venmo for its convenience—you can set transactions to "public" (while keeping amounts private) so everyone can see how the funds are being used. To streamline team purchases, I've even signed up for a Venmo debit card, which keeps everything organized in one account.

A clear, upfront budget helps parents feel confident and invested. It allows them to see how their contributions enhance their child's experience while ensuring everyone is on the same page. Keep in mind that families' financial situations vary. Some parents may pay in full immediately, while others might contribute smaller amounts over time, such as $5, $10, or $20 when they can. Patience and understanding go a long way. Sending friendly reminders throughout the season helps keep everyone on track.

Here's How I Set My Budget:

- **Plan for Key Expenses:**
  - Uniforms and equipment
  - Snacks, drinks, and team dinners
  - End-of-season gifts for players and coaches
  - App subscriptions, like TeamSnap (it's worth every penny!)
  - Decorations and venue rentals for the end-of-season banquet
- **Identify Income Sources:**
  - Player fees or team donations
  - Fundraising efforts (more on this in a minute)
  - Community sponsorships or partnerships
- **Keep Track:**
  - I use a simple spreadsheet and keep two envelopes in my team binder: one for receipts and one for any cash or checks I collect. Venmo and PayPal are great for digital payments but always log those too.

Collecting Payments

This part can feel a little awkward, but making it simple and straightforward helps a lot:

- **Digital Options:** Venmo and PayPal are lifesavers. I even use a Venmo debit card for team purchases, so everything stays neat and transparent.
- **Cash or Check:** Old-school works too! Just jot down who paid and when in your log.
- **Be Patient:** Some families may need time to pay. I've had parents bring me $5 or $10 whenever they could, and it always worked out in the end. This doesn't mean you shouldn't stay on people about getting their fees paid, but foster open communication so you know whether to be empathetic or aggressive when it comes to collecting.

Supporting Families in Need

Not every family can afford the extra costs, and that's okay. Participating in sports can be an expensive proposition these days, especially in communities where youth sports may as well be the minor leagues. Here are some ways to make sure every kid gets to participate regardless of the economics:

- **Quiet Support:** I've reached out to parents who I knew could pitch in a little extra to cover for a family in need. Most people are more than happy to help.

- **Community Fundraising:** Social media can work wonders. Posting pictures of the team and asking for support from friends and family has helped us raise hundreds of dollars in the past.

Pro Tip: Be Discreet. Handle these situations privately to avoid embarrassment. The goal is to make everyone feel supported.

The *Other* "F-Word:" Fundraising

Fundraising is another great way to pull in team funds. I always joke that fundraising is every parent's least favorite "F" word. Fundraising isn't fun, but for some teams, it is a necessary evil and the best way to offset costs. Here are some ideas that have worked for us:

- **Swag Sales:** Hoodies, cups, and blankets with the team's logo are always a hit.

- **Touchdown Bucket:** Pass around a bucket during games after every score. You'd be amazed how quickly the dollars add up.

- **Classic Car Washes:** It's a tried-and-true method for a reason.

- **Bake Sales or Concessions:** Selling snacks at games can bring in a surprising amount of money.

- **Spirit Nights:** Partner with local restaurants for a percentage of the night's sales to go to the team.

Pro Tip: There are a million and one fundraising companies out there with their hands raised to help you collect cash for your team. But pay attention to the fine print. If these vendor partners don't take a fee, they are taking a cut. I've seen percentages as high as 60% percent, meaning for every hundred you raise, they are keeping $60 bucks! On occasion that deal might make sense (expensive product, a done for you service, etc.) but remember every dollar you give up keeps you further from your objectives.

Keeping It Transparent

Parents trust you with their money, so keeping things clear and organized is essential:

- **Include Parents and Coaches when Planning:** Get coaches and parents involved from the jump. Share a budget proposal early on and get feedback. Once it's settled, distribute it to the team to make sure everyone knows what is coming in and how it's being spent from day one.

- **Regular Updates:** Share financial updates at team meetings or through email. A quick "here's where we are" goes a long way.

- **Save Everything:** Keep receipts for every purchase. It's tedious, but you'll be glad you did if questions arise.

- **Don't Muddle Funds:** Do your best to keep team fees out of your personal accounts. Whether you setup dedicated accounts or keep cash in an envelope, the more you can do to be transparent about money coming in and money going out, the better off you'll be.

- **Plan for the Unexpected:** Always have a small contingency fund for last-minute needs, like extra gear or emergency snacks.

Wrapping It All Up

At the end of the season, provide a breakdown of all income and expenses. If there's leftover money, decide as a group how to use it: rolling it into next year's budget, refunding parents, or putting it toward a special team gift are all reasonable options.

Managing the finances might not be the most glamorous part of being a Team Mom, but it's absolutely one of the most important. And hey, you're doing an amazing job keeping everything running smoothly.

Never, never, never, mix business with pleasure. Or in this case team fees with your personal finances!

People may want to know how collected funds are being distributed. By accounting separately for team money, you'll be able to quickly show and tell if it comes up.

Team Mom
PLAYBOOK

Team Unity

Fostering a Sense of Family

A united team is an unstoppable team. When players, coaches, and parents feel like family, they'll bring that bond onto the field, creating something truly special. Building team unity requires intentional effort, and as Team Mom, you're the glue that holds it all together. From tear-away banners to team dinners, these efforts foster connection and pride.

Tear-Away Banners

A tear-away banner at halftime or during pregame introductions adds excitement and builds team spirit. Here's how to create one:

- **Materials:** Vinyl banners with Velcro down the middle work best. They're reusable and cost-effective.

- **Assembly:** Add grommets to the banner's corners and thread PVC pipes through for easy holding. Rope the grommets securely to keep the banner taut.

To simplify your life, this playbook includes a sample layout and assembly instructions. Most sign shops can print the banners, but in our experience they won't do the assembly. If needed, look to parents on the team, or friends and family for help with the stitching, stringing, and cutting.

Pro Tip: Include your team's slogan or mascot to personalize your banner. Use a local sign or print shop like **AlphaGraphics**, or **Fedex Office Print & Ship Center** to ensure quality results.

Roster Cards

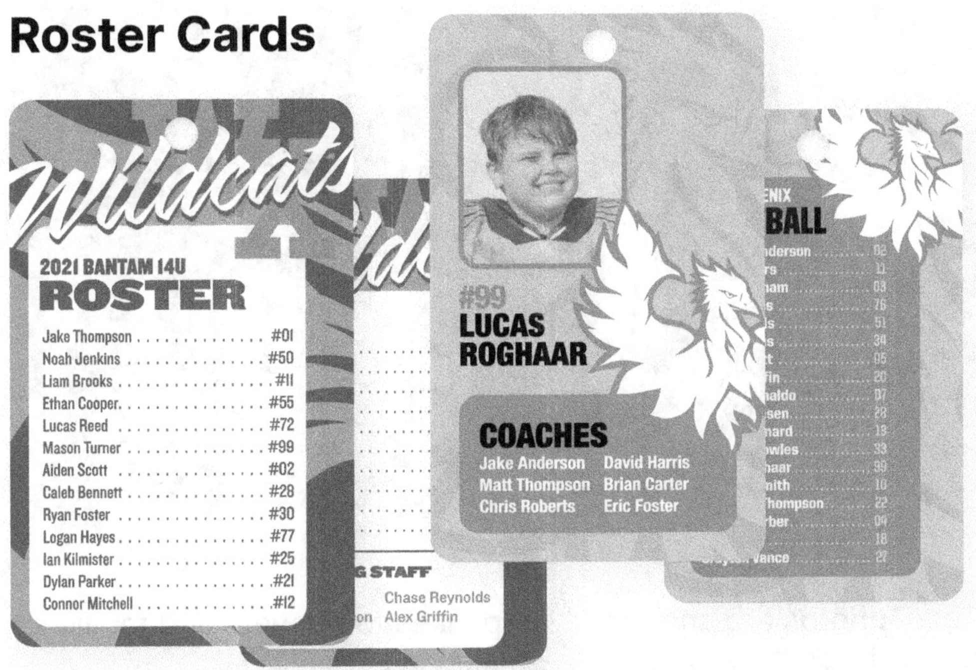

Early in the season, parents may not know every player's name. Roster cards help everyone cheer for the whole team:

- **Design:** Include the roster on one side and the schedule on the other.

- **Printing:** Print cards at a local shop and attach them to inexpensive lanyards from Amazon.

- **Impact:** Hearing their name from the stands boosts players' confidence and makes them feel appreciated.

Making Noise

Nothing pumps up players like a tunnel of cheering fans. Here are some ways to create that electric atmosphere:

- **Cowbells and Streamers:** Hand out team-colored cowbells or streamers to parents and siblings. Amazon has affordable options.

- **Smoke Bombs:** Smoke Effect sells vibrant smoke bombs that make for epic entrances. Check if your field allows them first.
- **Quick Setup:** Use kabob sticks or knitting needles to pass streamers quickly between parents, making setup a breeze.

Team Photos

Team photos are cherished keepsakes for players and families alike. Here's how to make them special:

- **Hire a Photographer:** If your league doesn't provide one, find a local photographer through apps like Thumbtack.
- **Memory Wall:** Display team photos at the end-of-season banquet or share them digitally through your team app.

Encouraging Unity

Beyond the physical items, unity is built through shared experiences and a supportive culture. Here are some additional ideas:

- **Create Team Traditions:** Start a pre-game chant or post-game huddle. Rituals like these build camaraderie and pride.
- **Celebrate Milestones:** Recognize individual and team achievements, from a first touchdown to a successful fundraiser. Hand out certificates or small tokens to mark these moments.

- **Plan Inclusive Events:** Host activities that involve the whole family, such as picnics, hikes, or volunteer days. This strengthens the bond between parents, players, and coaches.

- **Resolve Conflicts Constructively:** Encourage open communication and address any disagreements promptly and fairly. A positive atmosphere starts with mutual respect.

- **Support Everyone:** Be mindful of parents or players who may feel left out. Small gestures, like a friendly conversation or extra encouragement, can make a big difference.

Why It Matters

Unity transforms a team from a group of individuals into a cohesive force. It's what turns games into unforgettable experiences and creates lifelong memories for players and families alike. By prioritizing connection and camaraderie, you'll ensure the season is not only successful but meaningful for everyone involved.

Challenging Situations

Navigating Tough Moments

Sports seasons bring plenty of highs, but they can also come with challenges. As Team Mom, you're often the first point of contact when things get tough. Whether it's addressing an injured player, supporting a grieving family, or managing parental conflicts, your role is to help the team weather the storm and stay united.

Supporting Families During Difficult Times

Life doesn't pause for football, and players or their families may face personal hardships during the season. Whether it's an injury, illness, financial hardship, or the loss of a loved one, these challenges can take a toll both on and off the field. A strong team culture extends beyond the game, offering support when it's needed most. Coaches, parents, and teammates can rally around families to provide comfort, assistance, and encouragement. Small gestures can make a significant difference in helping someone feel seen and supported.

Here are a few meaningful ways to lend a hand:

- **Honoring Loss:** If a teammate loses a loved one, consider a gesture to show the team's support. Stickers on helmets, signed cards, or a bouquet (flower or candy) can mean the world to grieving families. For boys, a chocolate bouquet with heartfelt notes has been a popular choice.

- **Providing Meals:** For families dealing with injuries, surgeries, or illnesses, organizing meal deliveries can be a tremendous help. Use SignUp Genius to schedule contributions from parents.

- **Special Gifts:** We've had a few season ending injuries over the years and without exception the team and parents have rallied around the player to let them know that they are still a part of the crew — whether or not they are playing. We always encourage players and parents to keep coming to games, practices, and team events through the season to reinforce their continued inclusion in the "family."

Additionally, if the team has extra funds, or if you are able to take up a purpose-driven collection, consider gifting an injured player something meaningful, like a team blanket or custom gear. Small gestures make a big impact.

Offering Rides & Assistance: Some families may struggle with transportation due to unexpected circumstances. Coordinating rides to and from practice or helping with errands can ease their burden.

Addressing Parental Conflicts

Unfortunately, tensions can arise among parents. Your role as Team Mom may include diffusing these situations to protect the team atmosphere. Here's how:

- **Set Clear Expectations:** At the start of the season, share a code of conduct for sideline behavior. This gives you a framework to address issues if they arise.

- **Stay Neutral:** When conflicts occur, listen to both sides without taking sides. Focus on finding a solution that prioritizes the team's harmony.

- **Bring in Leadership:** If tensions escalate, involve the coach or league officials to mediate. Your priority is maintaining a positive environment for the players.

Dealing with Verbal or Physical Abuse

If you witness a parent or player displaying abusive behavior, it's essential to act quickly and appropriately:

- **Verbal Abuse on the Sidelines:** Politely remind parents of the team's expectations and the importance of setting a good example. If necessary, involve the coach to address persistent issues.

- **Abuse Towards Players:** For serious concerns, prioritize the child's safety. Report the behavior to the league and, if required, local authorities. Your role is to advocate for the well-being of all players.

Never interject in a situation that is violent or looks like it could become violent — *for parents or players.*

If a situation could get out of hand bring backup. Involve the appropriate authorities for the situation and if you aren't sure, include coaches or even police in any intervention.

Navigating Unexpected Events

From sudden weather changes to pandemic disruptions, flexibility is key:

- **Have a Backup Plan:** Be ready to adjust schedules or relocate events when necessary. Communicate changes promptly to avoid confusion.

- **Focus on Team Morale:** Keep spirits high during challenging times. Organize a fun, impromptu activity or send encouraging messages through your team app.

Building Resilience

Tough moments can bring a team closer together if handled with care and empathy. Encourage players to support each other during difficult times. Remind them that being part of a team means celebrating the highs and lifting each other during the lows.

Why Your Role Matters

Handling hard situations isn't easy, but it's an essential part of creating a safe, supportive environment for players and families. Your leadership sets the tone, showing that even during challenges, the team's unity and well-being come first.

Team Mom
PLAYBOOK

End of Season Festivities

Celebrating the Journey

The end of the season is a time to reflect, celebrate, and bring everyone together one last time. A well-planned end-of-season event recognizes the players' hard work, the coaches' dedication, and the parents' support. It's a chance to wrap up the season on a high note and leave everyone with cherished memories.

Planning an End-of-Season Banquet

In my years of team momming, we've always capped off the season with an end-of-season banquet. It is the grand finale—a celebration of all the hard work, growth, and memories created throughout the season. We normally relegate the invitation to the player and parents only, but it's your event! If you have the space, the budget, or the interest in extending the offer to siblings, grandparents, etc. go for it. After all, we're all one big, happy, extended football family.

If a team banquet is something you'd like to implement yourself, here's some ways to make it unforgettable:

- **Secure a Venue Early:**

  - Popular venues like community centers, banquet halls, or local restaurants fill up fast. Book as early as possible to lock in your preferred location.

  - Consider the vibe you want: a casual pizza party at a park, a sit-down dinner at a restaurant, or a themed event at a community center.

- **Set the Tone:**

  - Decide if the banquet will be casual or formal. For younger teams, a laid-back pizza party with games might be perfect. For older teams, a more polished even with speeches and awards could be a hit.

  - Create a theme if you want to add some extra fun. For example, a "Hollywood Night" where players walk a red carpet or a "Team Awards Show" with trophies and certificates.

- **Plan the Budget:**

  - Account for food, decorations, awards, and any extras like photo slideshows and venue costs. Share costs with parents early in the season to avoid last-minute surprises.

  - If funds are tight, consider a potluck-style banquet where parents contribute dishes.

Decorating on a Budget

Make your banquet festive without breaking the bank! A little creativity goes a long way in setting up a memorable and meaningful event while keeping costs low. Here are some budget-friendly ways to create a great atmosphere:

- **Team Colors:** Stick to your team's colors for balloons, tablecloths, and banners. The Dollar Store and Dollar Tree are great resources for affordable options. Consider mixing solid-colored decorations with patterned or textured pieces for a more polished look.

- **Photo Displays:** Create a photo wall showcasing highlights from the season. Use string lights or clothespins for an easy, creative setup. If printing large photos is too costly,

We have printed our annual custom hoodiesy with **Custom Ink** for nearly ten years. They have always produced high-quality, fairly-priced items for our teams and I'd have no problem recommending them to teams that want to print anything really.

create a digital slideshow to play on a screen throughout the banquet.

- **DIY Centerpieces:** Fill mason jars or simple vases with items like mini footballs, pom-poms, or LED candles. You can also use player photos, team logos, or small trophies as inexpensive yet meaningful table decorations.

- **Player Recognition Table:** Dedicate a space for awards, senior spotlights, or player shout-outs. Print out fun facts, stats, or favorite memories on cardstock to display.

- **Budget-Friendly Backdrop:** Create a simple photo booth using a themed backdrop made from a plastic tablecloth, streamers, or a fabric sheet in team colors. Add props like football helmets or foam fingers for fun photos.

- **Repurpose Past Decorations:** Check with parents or the school to see if any previous event decorations can be reused. Banners, table runners, and signage from previous banquets or pep rallies can often be repurposed.

Food Options

Teenagers are always hungry, so food is a critical part of any celebration. Consider these approaches:

- **Potluck Style:** Ask parents to bring dishes to share. Use a sign-up sheet to avoid duplicates.

- **Catered or Restaurant Meals:** Work with local restaurants for a group discount. Options like pizza or pasta are usually crowd-pleasers.

- **Themed Buffets:** Taco bars or baked potato bars are easy to set up and customizable for dietary preferences.

Adding Personal Touches

- **Slideshow or Video:** Compile photos and clips from the season, set to music, and play it during the banquet. Players love seeing themselves in action.

- **Highlight Speeches:** Keep speeches short but meaningful. Allow coaches, captains, or parents to share memorable moments or thank the team.

- **Team Awards:** Present fun awards like "Best Touchdown Dance" or "Most Improved" to make the night memorable.

Players' Gifts

Giving players a small token of appreciation is a wonderful way to commemorate the season. Here are a few ideas:

- **Memory Collages:** Collect photos from the season and create a collage for each player. Use affordable frames from Amazon for a polished finish.

- **Custom Hoodies:** Design a hoodie with the team name, mascot, and roster. These have been our annual giveaway as long as my sons have played football, and they are always a player favorite. Websites like Custom Ink or JakPrints offer reliable and affordable options. The odds are that you have a t-shirt shop in your community that can help out as well if you'd rather shop local.

- **Keepsake Plaques:** Present each player with a personalized plaque celebrating their contribution to the team.

- **DIY Gifts:** If you're crafty, consider making something special, like a wooden football-shaped keychain or a framed team photo with a handwritten note.

- **Custom Dog Tags or Keychains:** Personalized dog tags or keychains with the player's number, name, and team motto make for a great keepsake they can carry year-round. These can often be ordered in bulk for a reasonable price.

- **Signed Football or Mini Helmets:** Have coaches and teammates sign a football or mini helmet as a memento. This is a great option for seniors or players moving on to a new chapter.

- **Highlight Reel USB Drive:** Compile the best moments from the season into a highlight reel and load it onto a USB drive for each player. This makes for a memorable keepsake they can look back on for years.

Recognizing Coaches

Coaches pour their time and energy into the team, often without much recognition. They sacrifice hours of their time—away from their families and personal lives—to develop players, strategize for games, and instill valuable life lessons. Their impact goes far beyond the scoreboard, shaping young athletes into disciplined, hardworking individuals. Whether it's their first year coaching or their twentieth, a small gesture of gratitude can mean a lot. Here are some thoughtful ways to thank them:

- **Custom Mugs or Tumblers:** Personalize them with the team's logo and a heartfelt message.

- **Team Photo Gifts:** A framed team photo or collage makes a meaningful keepsake.

- **Group Card or Plaque:** Have all the players sign a card or create a plaque with a thank-you message from the team.

- **Personalized Playbook or Clipboard:** A customized clipboard or notebook with the coach's name and a team slogan is both practical and sentimental.

- **Gift Cards to a Favorite Restaurant or Coffee Shop:** Pool funds from parents to give a gift card to a place the coach enjoys—whether it's a steakhouse, coffee shop, or sporting goods store.

- **Signed Football or Helmet:** Have players sign a football or mini helmet as a lasting keepsake from the season.

- **Coaching Survival Kit:** Put together a fun package with essentials like a whistle, energy bars, pain relief patches, and a custom water bottle.

- **Custom Jersey or Hoodie:** Order a jersey or hoodie with "Coach" and their name on the back, making them an honorary part of the team.

- **Video Tribute:** Create a short video with players sharing their favorite memories, lessons learned, or funny moments from the season.

Ending on a High Note

The end of the season isn't just about closing a chapter— it's about celebrating the journey, the friendships, and the memories made along the way. After a night of reflection, recognition, and gratitude, bring everyone together for one final team huddle. Encourage players, parents, and coaches to gather in a circle, just like they did before every game, to share one last moment as a team.

Coaches can offer final words of encouragement, seniors can share parting thoughts, and younger players can look ahead to the future. End with a powerful team cheer—whether it's the school fight song, a rallying chant, or a simple "1-2-3 [Team Name]!"—to solidify the bonds built throughout the season.

To preserve the moment, capture a group photo of the entire team, coaches, and families. This picture can serve as a lasting reminder of the hard work, dedication, and camaraderie that defined the season. Consider printing and sharing the photo with families or using it in next year's banquet slideshow to continue the tradition..

Why It Matters

A thoughtful end-of-season celebration not only recognizes everyone's contributions but also builds anticipation for next year. It's the perfect way to leave a lasting impression and foster team spirit that carries into the next season.

Section VIII

What's Next

43

Laying the Foundation for Future Success

As the current season winds down, it's the perfect time to start thinking about the next. A little preparation now will make next year's kickoff smoother and more exciting. By staying proactive, you'll maintain the momentum you've built and set the stage for an even better experience.

Off-Season Engagement

Just because the season is over doesn't mean the team spirit has to fade. Here's how to keep everyone connected and engaged during the off-season:

- **Stay Connected:** Create a group chat or social media group to keep players and parents in touch. Share updates, motivational posts, and training tips.

  - Use platforms like **TeamSnap** or **Band** to maintain communication and share resources.

- **Casual Meet-Ups:** Organize occasional off-season get-togethers, like a bowling night, a park day, or a team barbecue. These events keep the team bond strong and maintain enthusiasm.

- **Skill Development:** Encourage players to stay active and keep their skills sharp. Share information about local training camps, football clinics, or even online tutorials.

  - Organize informal practice sessions or scrimmages to keep players engaged and ready for the next season.

Early Feedback and Reflection

The off-season is the perfect time to gather feedback and reflect on what worked well—and what could be improved.

Here's how:

- **Survey the Team:** Send a simple survey to parents and players. Ask what they enjoyed about the season and what could be improved. Use tools like **Google Forms** or **SurveyMonkey** to make it easy.

  - Example questions: What was your favorite part of the season? What could we do better next year? Are there any activities or traditions you'd like to see added?

- **Coach Input:** Meet with the coaches to discuss the season. What worked well? What challenges did they face? Their insights are invaluable for planning next year.

  Use this time to brainstorm new strategies or ideas for team-building and skill development.

- **Parent Feedback:** Host a casual meeting or coffee chat with parents to gather their thoughts. What did they appreciate? What could be smoother? Their input can help you refine your approach.

Recognizing and Building on Successes

A season is much more than just wins and losses—it's about growth, perseverance, and the lessons learned along the way. Taking time to celebrate both team and individual accomplishments helps reinforce a positive culture and keeps players motivated for the future. Recognizing these successes doesn't have to be limited to the banquet; coaches and parents can find creative ways to highlight achievements throughout the off-season, keeping the team's momentum going.

Here are a few ways to acknowledge and build on this year's progress:

- **Highlight Achievements:** Did the team improve its record? Did players master new skills? Celebrate these milestones and share them with the team. Recognizing hard work fosters confidence and motivation for next season.

- **Create a "Season Highlights" Post or Video:** Compile footage from games, practices, and team bonding moments into a short video or social media post. Share it at the banquet, in the team group chat, or on social media to commemorate the season.

- **Recognize Individual Players:** Beyond the usual awards, consider highlighting unique contributions. Maybe a player showed great leadership, demonstrated resilience after an injury, or was always the first to lift up a teammate. Recognizing these qualities builds team spirit and reinforces the values that matter most.

- **Set Goals for Next Season:** Work with the coaches and players to identify areas for growth. These could include improving teamwork, mastering specific skills, or even just having more fun. Sharing these goals with parents keeps everyone aligned and motivated.

- **Encourage Reflection:** Ask players to think about their proudest moments from the season and what they want to work on next year. A simple survey or group discussion can help guide off-season preparation.

Early Organizational Planning

The off-season might seem far away, but getting a head start on planning can make next year's transition much smoother. A little preparation now can save countless hours of scrambling later. Whether it's organizing rosters, mapping out schedules, or recruiting volunteers, early planning sets the foundation for a well-run season. Here's how to stay ahead of the game:

- **Update Rosters:** Start gathering player and parent information for the next season. Having an up-to-date contact list early makes communication much easier, especially when planning off-season events.

- **Block Key Dates:** Tentatively schedule important dates like the first practice, team meetings, and fundraising events. Sharing these in advance allows families to plan ahead and ensures better attendance.

The league we play in has annual tryouts and then they select teams by skill level. This makes it hard to plan for next year's team in advance.

That said, the network you build now will follow you no matter the team so invest in great relationships!

46

- **Delegate Roles:** Start recruiting parent volunteers for next season. Assign roles like snack coordinator, fundraising lead, or team photographer to lighten your workload. The sooner roles are filled, the smoother next season will be.

- **Secure Facilities and Equipment:** If your team relies on specific practice fields, weight rooms, or training spaces, check on availability early. Also, take inventory of equipment to see what needs replacing.

- **Plan Off-Season Training Opportunities:** Whether it's optional strength training, summer camps, or informal meetups, having a rough idea of what's available keeps players engaged without overwhelming them.

Building Anticipation

The season may be over, but the excitement doesn't have to stop. Keeping the team spirit alive during the off-season ensures players stay connected and eager to return. A little bit of anticipation-building can go a long way in keeping morale high and reinforcing team unity. Here's how:

- **Share Sneak Peeks:** If you're planning any new initiatives or events, drop hints to get players excited. For example, "Next season, we're adding a new team-building activity—stay tuned!"

- **Highlight Returning Players:** Celebrate the players who are coming back for another season. Recognizing their dedication fosters team pride and builds excitement for the future.

- **Create a Countdown:** Use social media or your team app to count down to the first practice or game. Share fun facts, photos, or motivational quotes to build anticipation.

- **Keep the Team Engaged with Off-Season Challenges:** Friendly competitions—like workout challenges, skill drills, or trivia contests—can keep players involved without feeling like a chore.

- **Encourage Team Bonding:** Suggest casual get-togethers like pickup games, team hikes, or movie nights. Keeping relationships strong during the off-season makes the return to football even more exciting.

Encouraging Rest and Recovery

While staying engaged in the off-season is important, it's equally crucial to allow time for rest and recovery. Overtraining can lead to burnout, injuries, and a loss of passion for the game. Players need time to recharge both physically and mentally so they return refreshed and ready for the next season. Here's how to encourage a balanced approach:

- **Promote Rest:** Remind players and parents that the off-season is a time to relax and recover. Encourage players to explore other hobbies, spend time with family, and enjoy activities outside of football.

- **Avoid Burnout:** Too much focus on the sport can lead to fatigue and loss of enthusiasm. Help players strike a balance by encouraging light training while emphasizing the importance of fun and downtime.

- **Encourage Cross-Training:** Playing other sports or engaging in different types of physical activity—like swimming, basketball, or yoga—can help prevent injuries while keeping players in shape.

- **Support Mental Recovery:** The demands of the season can be intense, so the off-season is a great time for players to recharge mentally. Encourage activities that reduce stress, such as reading, music, or spending time outdoors.

- **Check in with Players:** Some athletes struggle with the transition to the off-season, especially seniors moving on to the next stage of their lives. Keeping an open line of communication ensures they feel supported, even after the final whistle blows.

Why This Matters

Preparing for the next season isn't just about logistics; it's about sustaining the team's energy and spirit. By taking proactive steps now, you'll make the transition seamless and keep everyone—players, parents, and coaches—excited for what's ahead.

Team Mom
PLAYBOOK

Ending on a High Note

A Heartfelt Thank You

As you wrap up your season and reflect on all the moments—the triumphs, the challenges, and the laughter—take a moment to acknowledge the incredible role you've played. Being a Team Mom isn't just about organizing schedules or arranging snacks; it's about creating an environment where players can thrive, parents feel connected, and everyone feels valued. Your dedication has made this possible, and that's something to celebrate.

Being a Team Mom is more than just a role—it's a calling. The impact you have on these players, their families, and the community will last far beyond the season. Your efforts help build not just better teams, but better individuals, teaching life lessons about teamwork, commitment, and resilience.

Thank you for stepping up, giving your time, and putting your heart into making this season unforgettable. Here's to many more seasons of teamwork, growth, and joy. **Go Team Moms**!

Team Mom
PLAYBOOK

Section X

Sample Documents

Team Mom
PLAYBOOK

Premium Form Access

Hey, Team Mom—you've got perks!

When you bought The Team Mom Playbook: Football Edition, you also unlocked access to premium digital versions of all the forms in the book. They're fillable, printable, and ready to help you run your season like a pro.

To get your free premium forms:

- [ ] Go to **teammomplaybook.com/premium-forms**
- [ ] Enter your **name, email address, and the access code printed below**
- [ ] Check your inbox—we'll send you a link to download your forms

That's it! Quick, easy, and **FREE** with your book purchase.

ACCESS CODE

BXGHDLQY

Pre-Season Checklist

Communication & Planning

- [ ] Set up communication channels (TeamSnap, GroupMe, email)
- [ ] Create a master calendar with all key dates
- [ ] Draft and share the team budget
- [ ] Send welcome email to parents with important info
- [ ] Schedule a pre-season parent meeting

Uniforms & Equipment

- [ ] Organize uniform fitting and distribution
- [ ] Order team gear (e.g., jerseys, pads, helmets, balls)
- [ ] Double-check equipment and supplies
- [ ] Set up a lost-and-found bin
- [ ] Prepare a first-aid kit

Logistics & Scheduling

- [ ] Confirm first practice details with coaches
- [ ] Confirm field reservations and game schedules

Finances

- [ ] Collect player fees and donations

Team Building & Volunteers

- [ ] Assign volunteer roles (snacks, fundraising, etc.)
- [ ] Plan and schedule team-building activities

Other

- [ ] _______________________________
- [ ] _______________________________
- [ ] _______________________________
- [ ] _______________________________
- [ ] _______________________________
- [ ] _______________________________
- [ ] _______________________________

Notes:

Download digital versions at:
teammomplaybook.com/premium-forms

Team Communication Plan Template

Primary Communication Method:

☐ TeamSnap

☐ Text Message/SMS

☐ Email

☐ Other: _______________

Backup Communication Method:

☐ Text

☐ Phone call

☐ Other: _______________

Key Contacts:

Head Coach: _________________________________ Phone: _______________

Assistant Coach: _________________________________ Phone: _______________

Equipment Manager: _________________________________ Phone: _______________

Team Mom: _________________________________ Phone: _______________

Snack Coordinator: _________________________________ Phone: _______________

Frequency of Updates:

☐ Weekly reminders

☐ Game-day alerts

☐ Monthly newsletters

☐ Other: _______________

Download digital versions at:
teammomplaybook.com/premium-forms

Team Budget

Item	Description	Amount
e.g. Team Meal Supplies	*Paper plates, utensils, napkins*	*$100*
	Total Budget	
	Cost per player (Team Fee)	

Download digital versions at:
teammomplaybook.com/premium-forms

Money Tracker

Team Income

Item	Player/Name	Amount	Total
e.g. Team Fee	J. Doe	$50	$50.00
e.g. Donation	Local Grocer	$100	$150.00
	Total Income		

Team Expenses

Item	Amount	Total
e.g. App Subscription	$50	$50.00
e.g. Pavillion Rental	$100	$150.00
Total Expenses		
Total Income minus Expenses		

Download digital versions at:
teammomplaybook.com/premium-forms

Snack Schedule

Date: 09/26	Game: *Falcons vs. Mountain Climbers*	
Snack:	**Half-Time Snack**	**Post-Game Snack**
Name:	*Julie Andrews*	*Frank Malone*
Contact #:	*(XXX)XXX-XXXX*	*(XXX)XXX-XXXX*

Date:	Game:	
Snack:	**Half-Time Snack**	**Post-Game Snack**
Name:		
Contact #:		

Date:	Game:	
Snack:	**Half-Time Snack**	**Post-Game Snack**
Name:		
Contact #:		

Date:	Game:	
Snack:	**Half-Time Snack**	**Post-Game Snack**
Name:		
Contact #:		

Healthy Snack Suggestions:

- ☐ Fresh Fruit (apples, oranges, bananas)
- ☐ Granola Bars
- ☐ Veggies and dips
- ☐ Cheese sticks
- ☐ Trail mix

Download digital versions at:
teammomplaybook.com/premium-forms

Team Dinner Schedule

Date: 10/21	Location: *Practice field north pavilion*	
	Name	**Contact**
Main	*Bea Arthur*	*(XXX)XXX-XXXX*
Side	*Betty White*	*(XXX)XXX-XXXX*
Drinks	*Estelle Getty*	*(XXX)XXX-XXXX*
Dessert	*Rue McClanahan*	*(XXX)XXX-XXXX*

Date:	Location:	
	Name	**Contact**
Main		
Side		
Drinks		
Dessert		

Date:	Location:	
	Name	**Contact**
Main		
Side		
Drinks		
Dessert		

Download digital versions at:
teammomplaybook.com/premium-forms

Volunteer Sign-Up

Assignment/Role	Name	Contact Information
e.g. Snack Coordinator	*Sally Fields*	**Email:** *sally@domain.com* **Phone:** *(XXX) XXX-XXXX*

Notes: *Will schedule snacks a week in advance.*

Assignment/Role	Name	Contact Information
		Email: **Phone:**

Notes:

Assignment/Role	Name	Contact Information
		Email: **Phone:**

Notes:

Assignment/Role	Name	Contact Information
		Email: **Phone:**

Notes:

Assignment/Role	Name	Contact Information
		Email: **Phone:**

Notes:

Example Assignments:

- ☐ Snack Coordinator
- ☐ Fundraising Lead
- ☐ Team Photographer
- ☐ Equipment Manager
- ☐ Team Dinner Coordinator

Download digital versions at:
teammomplaybook.com/premium-forms

Team Contact List

Player Name: *Jason Alexander*   **Jersey Number:** *74*

Parent/Guardian: *Daniel Andrews*	**Phone:** *(XXX)XXX-XXXX*	**Email:** *name@domain.com*
Parent/Guardian: *Julie Andrews*	**Phone:** *(XXX)XXX-XXXX*	**Email:** *name@domain.com*

Address: *123 Anystrevet Dr.*

Allergies/Notes/Etc.: *Avoid Pine Nuts*

Player Name: **Jersey Number:**

Parent/Guardian:	**Phone:**	**Email:**
Parent/Guardian:v	**Phone:**	**Email:**

Address:

Allergies/Notes/Etc.:

Player Name: **Jersey Number:**

Parent/Guardian:	**Phone:**	**Email:**
Parent/Guardian:	**Phone:**	**Email:**

Address:

Allergies/Notes/Etc.:

Download digital versions at:
teammomplaybook.com/premium-forms

Game Day Checklist

Pre-Game

- [ ] Confirm snacks are ready
- [ ] Check equipment (balls, cones, water)
- [ ] Bring/setup banners and decorations
- [ ] Confirm player attendance
- [ ] Verify that first aid and repair kits are on the sideline

Mid-Game

- [ ] Distribute half-time snacks
- [ ] Refill/replace water bottles
- [ ] Safety check equipment
- [ ] Take photos or videos

Post-Game

- [ ] Distribute post-game snacks
- [ ] Collect any loose or forgotten equipment and clothing
- [ ] Clean up sidelines and stands
- [ ] Update team apps with game results and other data
- [ ] Send reminders for upcoming week's games/practices

Other

- [ ] __________________________________
- [ ] __________________________________
- [ ] __________________________________
- [ ] __________________________________
- [ ] __________________________________
- [ ] __________________________________
- [ ] __________________________________

Notes:

Download digital versions at:
teammomplaybook.com/premium-forms

End-of-Season Banquet Planner

Venue

☐ Booked: ___________________________

Date: _______________

☐ Setup: Tables, Chairs, Decoration

Food & Drink

☐ Caterer: _______________________

Menu: _________________________

Drinks: ________________________

Quantity: ______________________

Decorations

☐ Team Colors _________________

☐ Balloons, banners, tablecloths

☐ _________________________

☐ _________________________

Awards & Gifts

☐ Player Awards/Gifts:

____

☐ Coach's Gifts:

____

☐ Certificates:

____

Volunteers

☐ Setup Crew:

____

☐ Cleanup Crew:

____

Other

☐ _________________________

☐ _________________________

☐ _________________________

☐ _________________________

☐ _________________________

☐ _________________________

☐ _________________________

Notes:

Download digital versions at:
teammomplaybook.com/premium-forms

End-of-Season Feedback Survey

Instructions:

Please rate the following on a scale from 1 to 10, where 1 = "Very Poor" and 10 = "Excellent."

Communication & Organization

How well did Team Leadership communicate important information during the season?

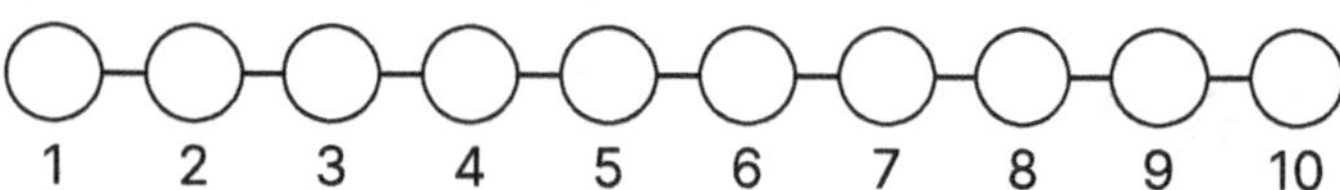

How effective were the tools used to communicate (e.g., TeamSnap, group texts, email)?

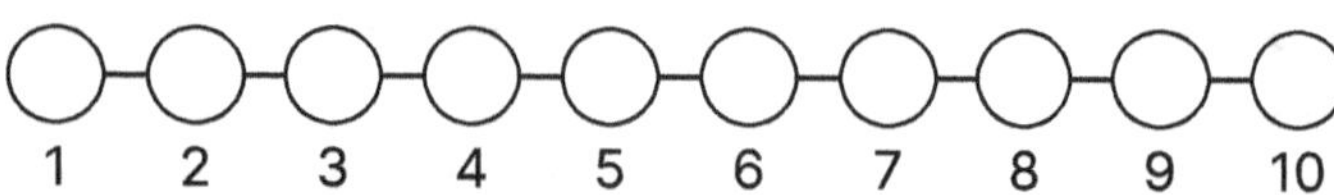

How organized did you feel the season was overall?

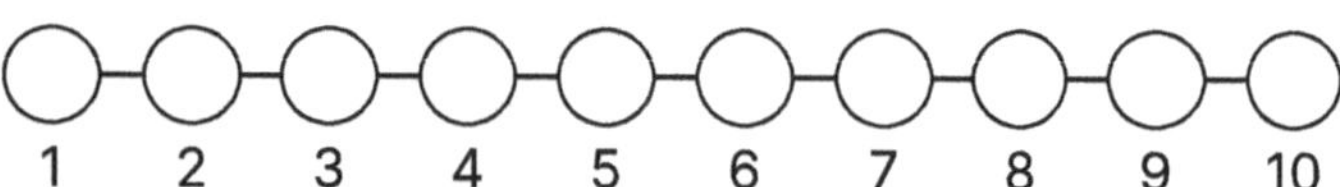

How clear were the expectations for snacks, volunteering, and events?

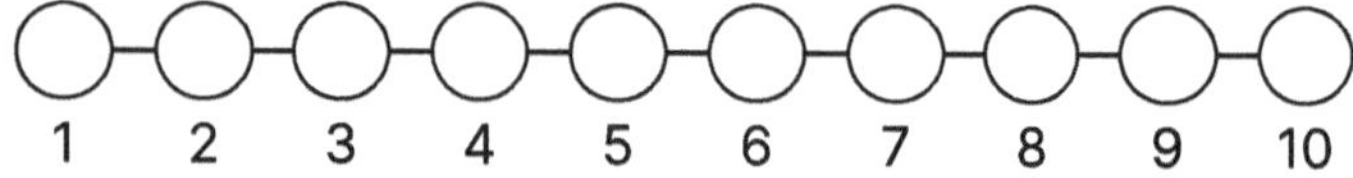

Game Day & Logistics

How smooth and well-managed were game-day logistics (snacks, equipment, setup)?

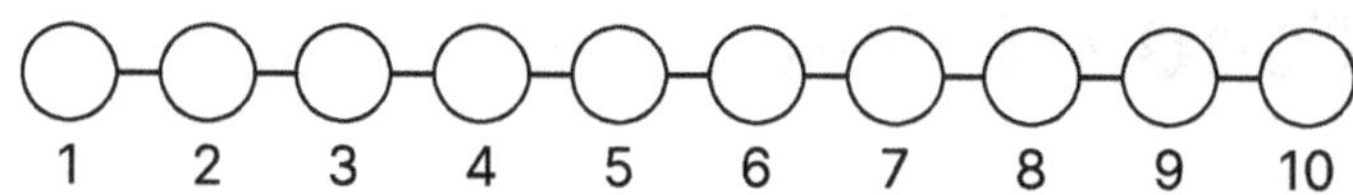

How well were uniforms, gear, and other essentials handled throughout the season?

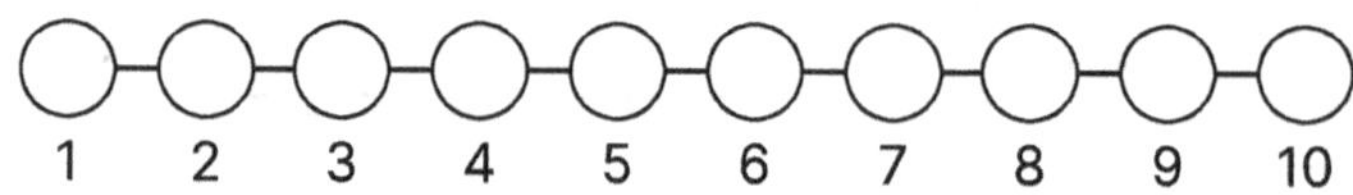

Team Bonding & Engagement

How would you rate the value and impact of team dinners?

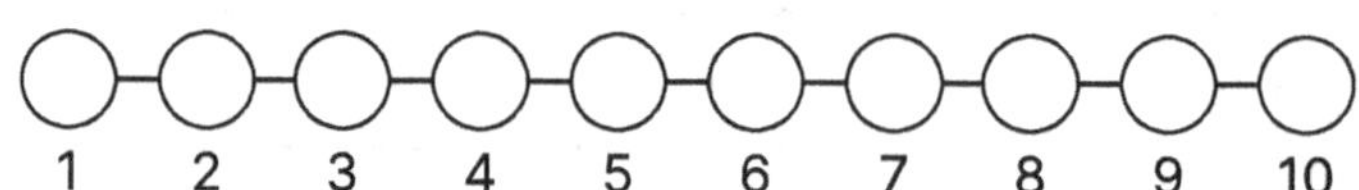

How successful were the team-building activities (e.g., BBQs, parties, family events)?

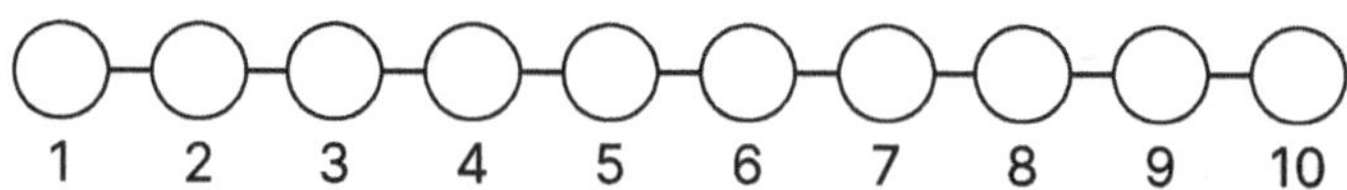

How inclusive did the team activities feel for all players and families?

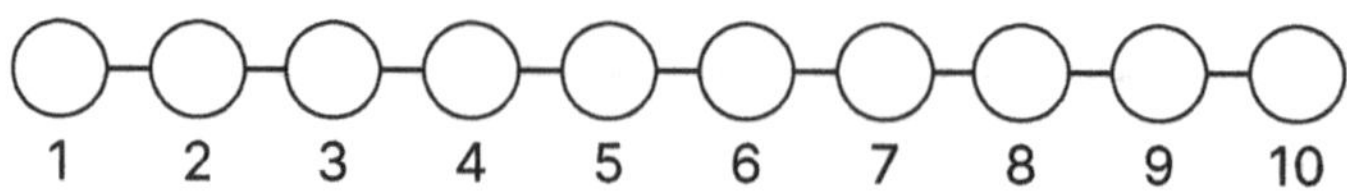

Download digital versions at:
teammomplaybook.com/premium-forms

Support & Responsiveness

How approachable was Team Leadership when questions or issues arose?

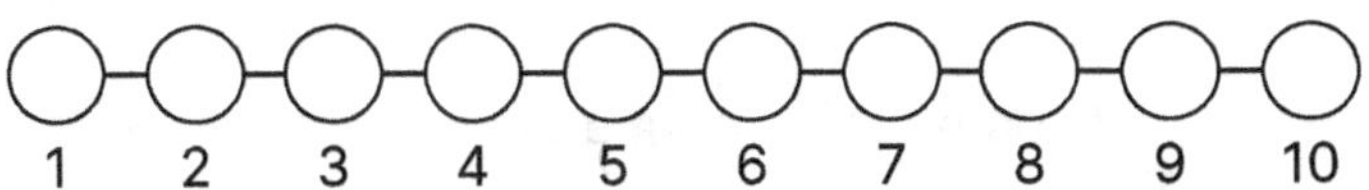

1   2   3   4   5   6   7   8   9   10

How well were families supported during the season (personal challenges, illness, injuries, etc.)?

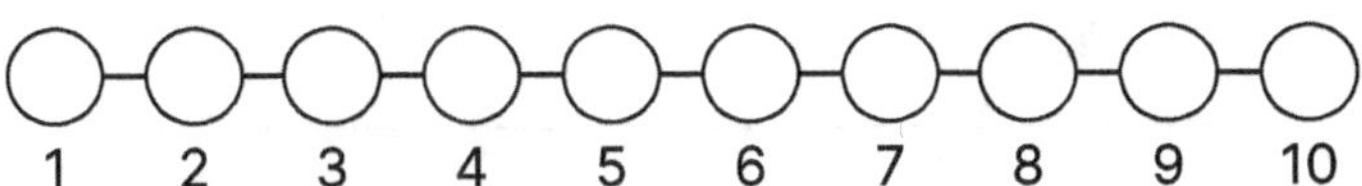

1   2   3   4   5   6   7   8   9   10

End-of-Season Celebration

How would you rate the end-of-season banquet/event in terms of planning and execution?

1   2   3   4   5   6   7   8   9   10

Overall Experience

How would you rate your overall experience with the team this season?

1   2   3   4   5   6   7   8   9   10

Open-Ended Feedback (Optional)

What was your favorite memory or highlight from this season?

____

____

____

____

____

____

Do you have any suggestions for improvement next season?

____

____

____

____

____

____

____

____

____

**Download digital versions at:
teammomplaybook.com/premium-forms**

Tear-Away Banner Design Template

140" (+1" Bleed on all sides)

74"

Grommets (1" from edge)

BANNER 1

BANNER 2

24"

4"

24"

Overlap

1" Bleed

Hook-and-loop fastener

74"

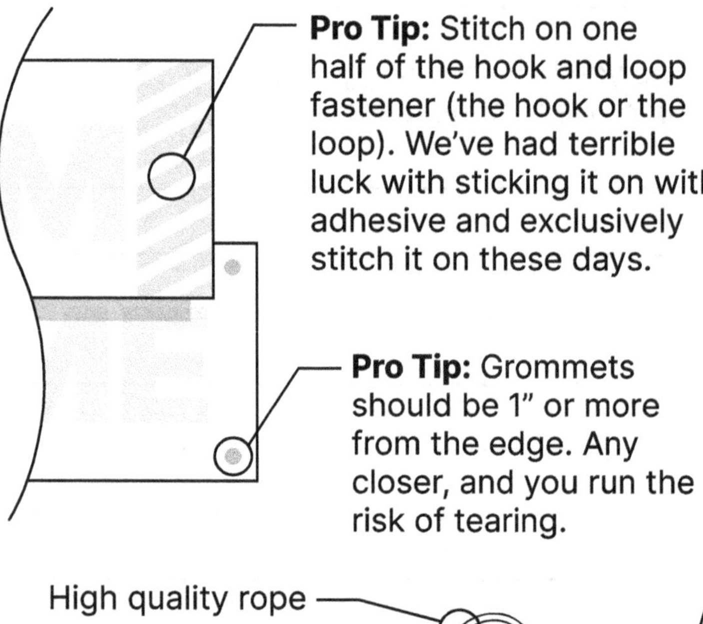

Pro Tip: Stitch on one half of the hook and loop fastener (the hook or the loop). We've had terrible luck with sticking it on with adhesive and exclusively stitch it on these days.

Pro Tip: Grommets should be 1" or more from the edge. Any closer, and you run the risk of tearing.

High quality rope

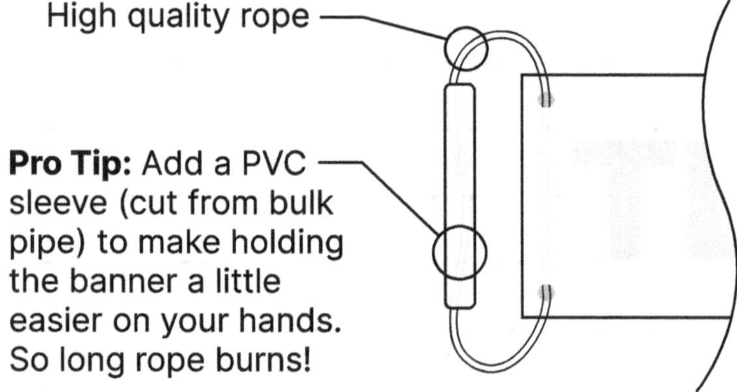

Pro Tip: Add a PVC sleeve (cut from bulk pipe) to make holding the banner a little easier on your hands. So long rope burns!

Commercial printers have a language all their own. In order to make sure that you get quality output at the print shop, we're including some sample specifications below for the example above as well as a list of supplies so you can take your tear-away banner to the next level.

Sample specs for your printer:

2× 24"×72" Banners — Full color one side with a 1" bleed on all sides.

4× Grommets — One in the top and bottom left corners of banner 1, and one in the top and bottom right of banner 2.

DIY supplies:

1× Stick of PVC pipe cut into "handles" for either end of the banner.

1× 4" wide hook-and-loop material

1× Length of high-quality rope

Download digital versions at:
teammomplaybook.com/premium-forms

Roster Card Design Template

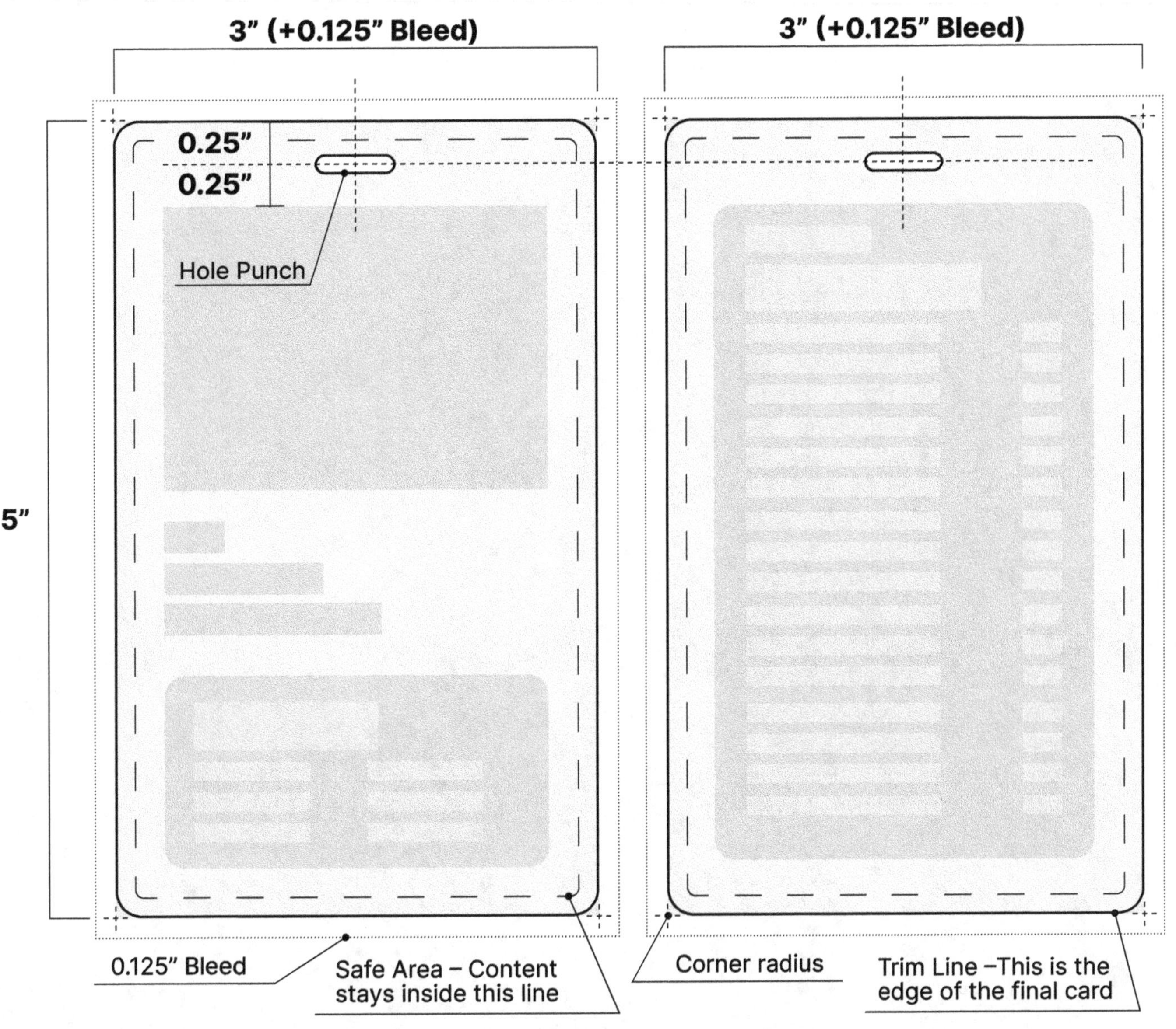

Commercial printers have a language all their own. In order to make sure that you get quality output at the print shop, we're including some sample specifications for the example above to take your roster cards to the next level.

Sample specs for your printer:

3"×5" Card — Full color both sides with a 0.125" bleed on all sides. Rounded corners and a hole punch at the top.

Pro Tip: Print these cards on waterproof and tear resistant synthetic paper and there will be no need to laminate. Every bit as durable and usually less costly!

Download digital versions at:
teammomplaybook.com/premium-forms

Team Mom
PLAYBOOK

Team Mom
PLAYBOOK

Team Mom
PLAYBOOK

9 780982 458747